EARTH'S TWIN?
THE PLANET VENUS

BY ISAAC ASIMOV
WITH REVISIONS AND UPDATING BY FRANCIS REDDY

Gareth Stevens Publishing
MILWAUKEE

For a free color catalog describing Gareth Stevens' list of high-quality books, call 1-800-542-2595 (USA) or 1-800-461-9120 (Canada). Gareth Stevens' Fax: (414) 225-0377.

Library of Congress Cataloging-in-Publication Data

Asimov, Isaac.
 Earth's twin? the planet Venus / by Isaac Asimov; with
revisions and updating by Francis Reddy.
  p. cm. — (Isaac Asimov's New library of the universe)
 Rev. ed. of: Venus: a shrouded mystery. 1990.
 Includes index.
 Summary: Describes the characteristics of the planet Venus and how
we discovered them.
 ISBN 0-8368-1233-6
 1. Venus (Planet)—Juvenile literature. [1. Venus (Planet)]
I. Asimov, Isaac. Venus: a shrouded mystery. II. Reddy, Francis, 1959-.
III. Title. IV. Series: Asimov, Isaac. New library of the universe.
QB621.A82   1996
523.4'2—dc20   95-40365

This edition first published in 1996 by
Gareth Stevens Publishing
1555 North RiverCenter Drive, Suite 201
Milwaukee, Wisconsin 53212, USA

Project editor: Barbara J. Behm
Design adaptation: Helene Feider
Editorial assistant: Diane Laska
Production director: Teresa Mahsem
Picture research: Matthew Groshek and Diane Laska

Printed in the United States of America

1 2 3 4 5 6 7 8 9 99 99 98 97 96

To bring this classic of young people's information up to date, the editors at Gareth Stevens Publishing have selected two noted science authors, Greg Walz-Chojnacki and Francis Reddy. Walz-Chojnacki and Reddy coauthored the recent book *Celestial Delights: The Best Astronomical Events Through 2001.*

Walz-Chojnacki is also the author of the book *Comet: The Story Behind Halley's Comet* and various articles about the space program. He was an editor of *Odyssey,* an astronomy and space technology magazine for young people, for eleven years.

Reddy is the author of nine books, including *Halley's Comet, Children's Atlas of the Universe, Children's Atlas of Earth Through Time,* and *Children's Atlas of Native Americans,* plus numerous articles. He was an editor of *Astronomy* magazine for several years.

CONTENTS

We live in an enormously large place – the Universe. It's just in the last fifty-five years or so that we've found out how large it probably is. It's only natural that we would want to understand the place in which we live, so scientists have developed instruments – such as radio telescopes, satellites, probes, and many more – that have told us far more about the Universe than could possibly be imagined.

We have seen planets up close. We have learned about quasars and pulsars, black holes, and supernovas. We have gathered amazing data about how the Universe may have come into being and how it may end. Nothing could be more astonishing.

The nearest to Earth of all the planets, Venus remained a mystery for a long time. It has such a thick layer of clouds that, for years, astronomers could see nothing of its surface. But with probes and other recent technology, more and more is being discovered about the shrouded planet, Venus.

Isaac Asimov

Venus – Only One Planet

Venus is the brightest of all the stars and planets in the sky. Only the Sun and the Moon are brighter. Unlike most planets, Venus never travels far from the Sun, and it can only be seen just before sunrise or just after sunset. When it is east of the Sun, Venus shines in the evening sky and is called the Evening Star. When it is west of the Sun, it shines before dawn as the Morning Star.

Ancient peoples thought the Morning Star and the Evening Star were two different objects. They even gave them different names. Today, we know they are one object, not two.

Because of its brightness, Venus was named after the Roman goddess of love.

Opposite: The Moon and Venus in a multiple-exposure photograph over Tulsa, Oklahoma.

Right: Venus, the Roman goddess of love.

5

Phases of Venus

The ancient Babylonians noticed Venus's motion in the sky and became interested in the motions of the other planets, too. This encouraged the early growth of the subjects of astronomy and mathematics.

Ptolemy, an ancient Greek astronomer, designed a method that predicted where Venus and the other planets would be in the sky at any given time. The only problem was that he pictured Earth as the center of our Solar System, instead of the Sun.

In the early 1600s, Italian astronomer Galileo Galilei studied Venus and found it had phases, like Earth's Moon. Sometimes it was full, sometimes half, sometimes just a crescent. The fact that Venus changed shape eventually helped prove that all the planets, including Earth, revolve around the Sun.

! ***Venus – a devil of a planet!***
The ancient Romans called Venus Lucifer, *which means "bringer of light." This was because when Venus, or the Morning Star, appeared, the Sun would soon follow. The king of Babylon was also called "the Morning Star." When the king was defeated in battle, the prophet Isaiah said, "How art thou fallen from heaven, O Lucifer, son of the morning!" People thought Isaiah was talking about the devil, cast out of heaven by God, so* Lucifer *became one of the names for the devil.*

The phases of Venus as recorded by astronomers in the eighteenth century *(opposite)* and the twentieth century *(below)*.

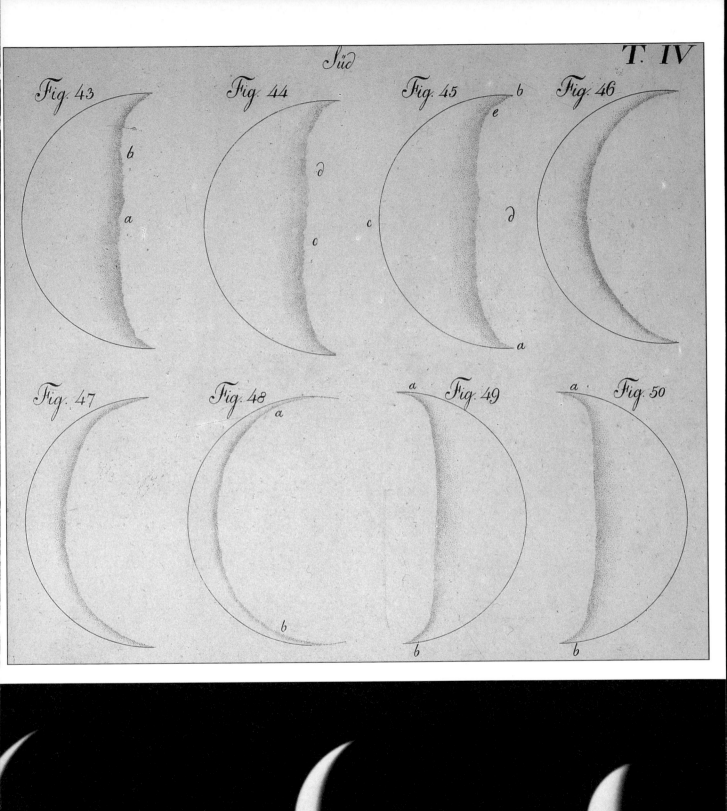

So Close, Yet So Far

When Venus is on the same side of the Sun as Earth, it can be as close to Earth as 23.7 million miles (38.1 million kilometers). This is closer than any other large celestial object except for our own Moon.

In 1761, an event called a solar transit occurred when Venus moved across the face of the Sun. By watching this and other transits of Venus across the Sun, astronomers could tell that Venus had an atmosphere.

When Venus is observed through a telescope, the only thing that can be seen is a dense cloud layer. For many years, this thick cloud cover kept astronomers from learning very much about Venus, even though Venus is the planet closest to Earth.

! *Now you see it, now you don't!*

What can be seen of Venus from Earth changes as Venus moves in its orbit. Our Moon is at its brightest when it is full. But when Venus is full, it is on the far side of the Sun, so it's harder for us to see. When Venus is nearest Earth, it looks like a thin crescent and usually gets lost in the twilight. The best time to view Venus is between these two phases, when it looks like a thick crescent.

Opposite: Heat-sensitive cameras reveal both the sunlit side of Venus *(white)* and warm clouds on the planet's night side *(yellow).*

Left and opposite, inset: In 1874, Venus moved across the face of the Sun. This solar transit gave astronomers their first chance to examine Venus's thick, cloudy atmosphere.

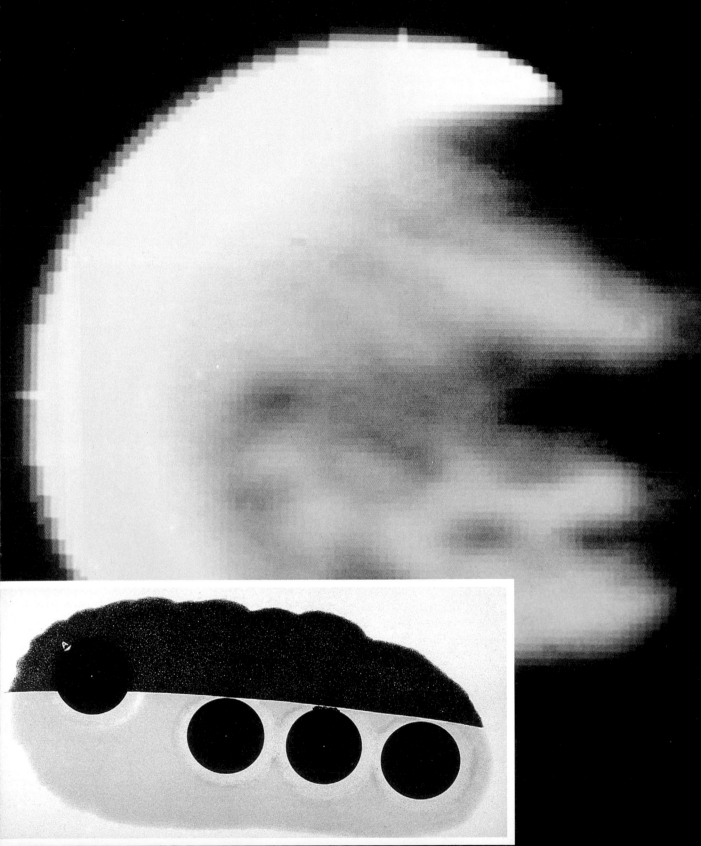

Earth's Twin?

Venus's thick cloud layer made many scientists think, at one time, that the planet must have water on its surface. Venus is closer to the Sun than Earth is. While this means Venus gets more heat than Earth, scientists thought Venus's clouds might reflect sunlight and keep the surface of the planet from getting too hot.

Some scientists and many science fiction writers once thought of Venus as a young planet. They imagined it looked like Earth in the prehistoric past, in the age of the dinosaurs. They pictured Venus as a tropical world with warm oceans and an abundance of plant and animal life. Since Venus is about the same size as Earth, many people looked upon it as Earth's twin.

! *Venus wins the all-around prize!*

The planets orbit the Sun in ellipses, which are lopsided orbits. Pluto's orbit is so lopsided that there is a difference of 1.4 billion miles (2.25 billion km) between its nearest and farthest distances from the Sun. Earth's orbit is much more circular, with a difference of only about 3 million miles (4.8 million km). But of all the planets, it is Venus, with a difference of about 1 million miles (1.6 million km), that has the orbit nearest to a perfect circle.

Opposite, top: In this artist's imagination, a distant volcano blasts a plume of dust and rock high above Venus's Asteria Regio region.

Left: Some people pictured Venus as a swampy world much like prehistoric Earth.

Above: Earth *(top)* is close in size to Venus *(bottom)*. Venus is only about 5 percent smaller than our planet.

11

Radio Waves from Venus

In the 1950s, astronomers began studying other kinds of radiation besides the waves of light. All objects give off electromagnetic radiation in the form of X rays, radio waves, ultraviolet, infrared, and light. Most of this radiation is not visible to the eye, but it can be detected with scientific instruments. What's more, objects with different temperatures give off different kinds of radiation. By measuring the type and amount of radiation an object emits, astronomers can determine its temperature.

In 1956, astronomers detected radio waves coming from Venus. This showed that Venus must be very hot – hotter than boiling water. Astronomers then knew that the cloud tops of Venus were hot. But they still couldn't tell the temperature on Venus's surface.

Right: Radio telescopes helped scientists determine the temperature of Venus.

Opposite: Like Earth, Venus probably has a hot core of liquid metal.

Inset: A heat-sensitive camera aboard the *Pioneer* probe pictured the clouds above the north pole of Venus. A dense, crescent-shaped cloud spirals outward 10 miles (16 km) above the main cloud deck. The bright spots are probably caused by rapidly moving clouds clearing away and exposing the warm atmospheric layers below.

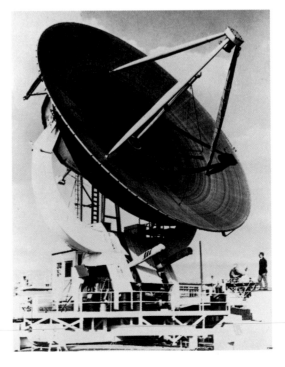
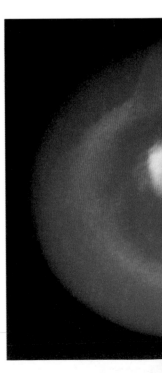

Hot and Heavy

Scientists realized there was only one way to find out more about Venus – to travel there. In 1961, the former Soviet Union sent the first of sixteen *Venera* probes to Venus. In 1967, *Venera 4* actually descended into Venus's atmosphere and sent back information to Earth. In 1970, *Venera 7* became the first probe to send back data from Venus's surface. *Mariner 2*, the first probe from the United States to study the planet, flew past Venus in 1962. Its instruments showed that the surface of Venus was indeed hot – at least 795° Fahrenheit (424° Centigrade). Scientists have since learned that Venus's surface is even hotter, at 864° F (462° C), hot enough to melt lead!

Venus's intense heat and incredible atmospheric pressure put the *Venera* probes out of action – but not before they sent back a wealth of information. They revealed that Venus's atmosphere is so thick that standing on the planet would feel like being at the bottom of an ocean. Scientists also learned that the atmosphere of Venus is made up almost entirely of carbon dioxide, with no oxygen. The lightning-filled clouds contain water mixed with sulfuric acid.

Top: An artist imagines lightning flashing in an orange Venusian sky.

Opposite, inset: In this drawing, a Soviet *Venera* probe is bathed in an eerie orange light on the surface of Venus.

Bottom: The surface of Venus as it was photographed by *Venera 13*. The image includes the bottom portion of the probe.

Earth and Venus: No Relation

The probes all showed one thing – Venus is not a twin sister of Earth. Except in size, the two planets are completely different. Venus is far too hot to have oceans of water or any form of Earthlike life. The surface of Venus is completely dry and desolate.

Venus's atmosphere is the opposite of Earth's. The air on Venus is 97 percent carbon dioxide and a little nitrogen. Earth's air is 78 percent nitrogen, 21 percent oxygen, and less than 0.1 percent carbon dioxide.

Heavy clouds reflect much of the sunlight falling on Venus, so its surface is always dim. Daylight on Venus is about the same as an overcast day on Earth. The clouds on Venus give sunlight an eerie orange color. The pressure of Venus's atmosphere is 93 times that of Earth's. Acid rain falls from the sky, but blistering heat evaporates the drops before they land!

! *Venus, the planet of 584 days!*

Venus moves around the Sun quicker than Earth does. Every 584 days, Venus gains a lap on Earth. Also, every 584 days, Venus is as close to Earth as it can get. Finally, Venus's rotation period is such that every 584 days it turns the same face to Earth. Some astronomers think Earth's gravity pulls at Venus and locks it into place. But Earth's gravity seems too weak for that. Could there be some other explanation? Scientists do not know for certain.

Right: Venus *(foreground)* as seen when nearest Earth. The Sun and Mercury are in the background.

Opposite: This illustration shows hot gases jetting through a vent in one of Venus's volcanoes.

Opposite, inset: In comparison, conditions on Earth *(pictured)* are quite different from those on Venus.

Answers in the Echoes

Mariner 2 discovered other surprises about Venus. By sending radio waves through the clouds to the surface of the planet and then recording the echoes, the probe discovered that Venus rotates very slowly. It takes Venus 243 days to make one turn on its axis, while Earth takes just 24 hours.

What's more, Venus rotates in the opposite direction of Earth. Earth and most of the other planets rotate counterclockwise, from west to east, but Venus rotates clockwise, from east to west.

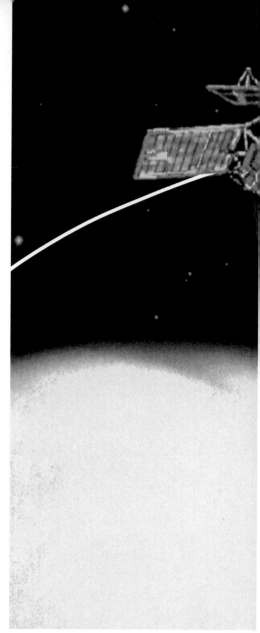

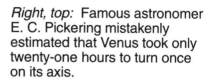

Right, top: Famous astronomer E. C. Pickering mistakenly estimated that Venus took only twenty-one hours to turn once on its axis.

Right, bottom: In 1951, R. M. Baum, an English astronomer observing Venus without the benefit of radio astronomy, determined the rotation of Venus to be 195 days.

Far right: In this illustration, *Mariner 2* determines Venus's correct length of rotation by bouncing radio waves off the planet's surface.

Inset: A more familiar version of the same procedure – at the rate of only one turn on its axis every 243 days, the planet Venus is not likely to receive a rotational speeding ticket!

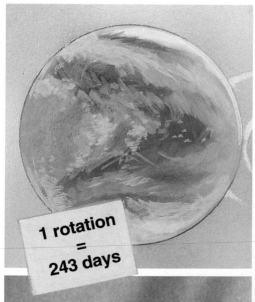

1 rotation = 243 days

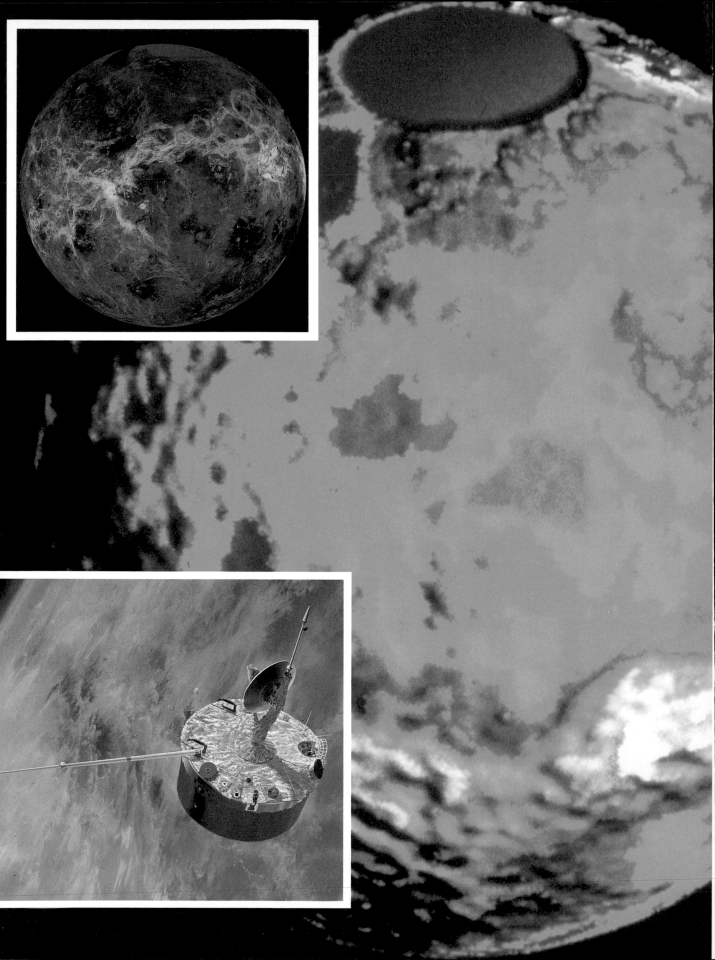

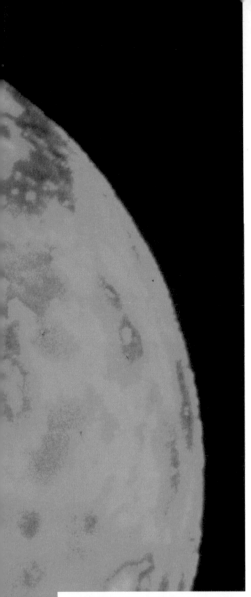

Mapping Venus

When radio waves are bounced off the surface of a planet, they reveal details of the planet's surface that are otherwise hidden.

Both the United States and the former Soviet Union have sent probes to Venus to map its surface through the use of radio waves. The most recent probe to undertake this mission is *Magellan* from the United States. It spent four years in orbit around Venus, mapping 98 percent of the planet's surface in great detail.

Left: Data from the U.S. *Pioneer Venus Orbiter* was used to make this early map of Venus. The north polar area *(top)* had not yet been mapped.

Opposite, top inset: This view of the surface of Venus was constructed with *Magellan* data that computers mapped onto a globe. The colors approximate those seen in images returned by the Soviet *Venera 13* and *14*.

The twisting bright features that cross the globe from the lower left toward the upper right are the mountains and canyons of the highland known as Aphrodite Terra.

Opposite, bottom inset: The *Pioneer Venus Orbiter* on the job mapping Venus.

Below: Magellan begins its journey to Venus.

Venus Revealed

As on Mercury, Mars, Earth, and the Moon, the terrain of Venus is divided into highlands and lowlands. Most of the highlands on Venus occur in just two regions – Ishtar Terra and Aphrodite Terra. These areas are similar to the continents of Earth. Ishtar Terra, in the north, is about the size of Australia and contains Maxwell Montes, the planet's highest mountain. Aphrodite Terra lies near the equator of Venus. It is about as big as Africa and features a series of winding canyons and highly fractured mountains.

By an agreement of the International Astronomical Union (IAU), all features on Venus are now given women's names. The IAU is the organization that approves the names given to features on the planets.

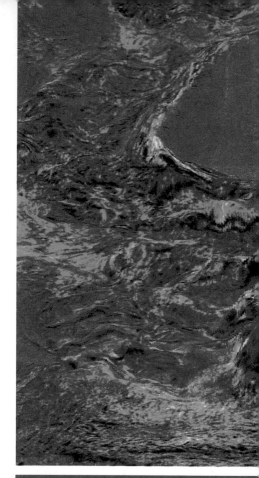

Top: Pictured is a pre-*Magellan* view of the region on Venus near the mountain Maxwell Montes *(orange area near bottom).* The mountains here rise 7 miles (11 km) above the surrounding terrain – that's taller than Mt. Everest on Earth.

Bottom: All of the data from *Magellan*'s visit to Venus went into making this map. The bright region is Maxwell Montes. Scattered dark patches are halos surrounding young impact craters.

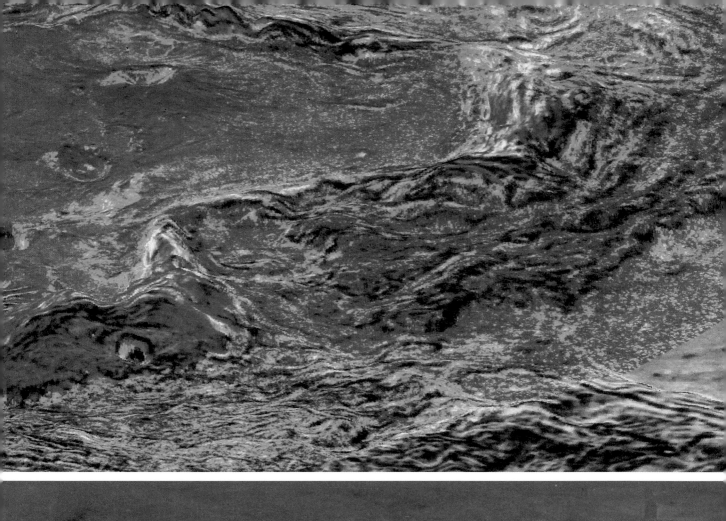

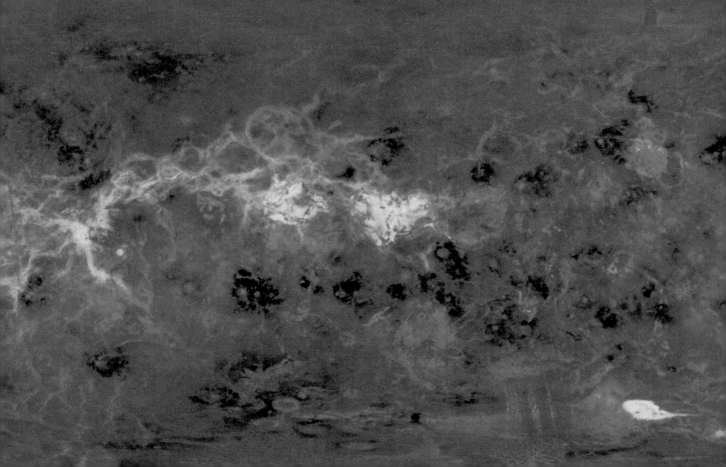

Craters and Coronae

Mercury, Mars, and the Moon are covered with thousands of impact craters that have accumulated over the last few billion years. Not so Venus – only about nine hundred craters have been identified. Many scientists think an intense period of volcanic activity took place on Venus 500 million years ago, filling the planet's oldest craters with lava.

In addition, scientists have recently found coronae on Venus. These are circular features marked by a ring of ridges. They seem to form when hot material from within the planet rises into the planet's crust, weakening the upper layers and bulging the surface. As the area cools, the bulge settles back down, leaving circular cracks around the edge of the bulge with cracks running straight across it. Such features may exist on Mars and possibly even in Earth's poorly mapped oceans – but they were found on Venus first!

Below, left: Meade is the largest impact crater known on Venus. It is 174 miles (280 km) across.

Below, right: The Pandora Corona measures 217 miles (350 km) across. The black stripes represent missing data.

Opposite: The volcano Sapas Mons rises in the center of this computer-generated view of *Magellan* data. Lava flows to the fractured plains in the foreground. The volcano, which is 249 miles (400 km) across and 0.9 miles (1.5 km) high, is located near Venus's equator. Color was artificially added and is based on the colors that the Soviet *Venera 13* and *14* observed.

One Theory – The Greenhouse Effect

It seems likely that Earth and Venus were more similar in the past than they are today. Venus now has no water on its surface and very little in its atmosphere, yet it may once have had oceans. If this is so, what changed it?

Because Venus is nearer the Sun than Earth is, Venus has always been warmer that Earth. Over time, more of its oceans could have evaporated, putting more water vapor into its atmosphere.

Water vapor holds in energy from the Sun. So Venus could have gotten still warmer, producing still more water vapor. Carbon dioxide in the oceans could have bubbled out as the water grew hotter. Carbon dioxide in the air also keeps heat from escaping. The temperature could have continued to rise until the oceans began to boil away caused by what is known as the "greenhouse effect." In the end, there would have been no oceans left, with a surface temperature as hot as a furnace.

The level of carbon dioxide in Earth's atmosphere has also been increasing. Scientists fear that, as a result, the temperature of Earth could slowly increase over the next few decades.

Opposite: The greenhouse effect may have occurred in Venus's cloudy atmosphere.

Inset: In an actual greenhouse on Earth, glass walls admit the warming rays of sunlight but keep infrared radiation, or heat, from leaving.

Top: Sunlight *(white lines)* reaches Venus, but gases in the atmosphere keep heat *(red lines)* from escaping.

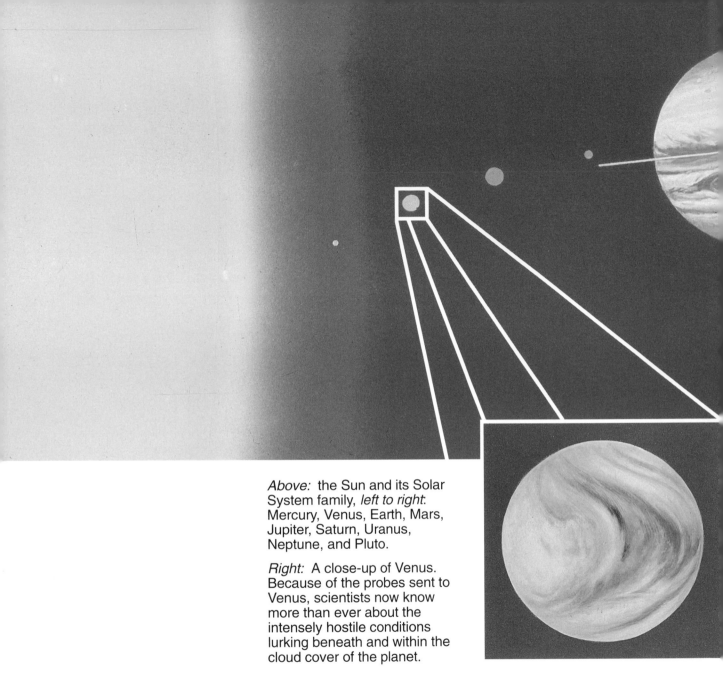

Above: the Sun and its Solar System family, *left to right:* Mercury, Venus, Earth, Mars, Jupiter, Saturn, Uranus, Neptune, and Pluto.

Right: A close-up of Venus. Because of the probes sent to Venus, scientists now know more than ever about the intensely hostile conditions lurking beneath and within the cloud cover of the planet.

Venus: How It Measures Up to Earth

Planet	Diameter	Rotation Period	Period of Orbit around Sun (length of year)	Known Moons	Surface Gravity	Distance from Sun (nearest-farthest)	Least Time It Takes Light to Travel to Earth
Venus	7,520 miles (12,101 km)	243 days*	224 days, 14 hours	None	0.88**	66.7-67.7 million miles (107.4-108.9 million km)	2 minutes, 6 seconds
Earth	7,925 miles (12,753 km)	23 hours, 56 minutes	365 days, 6 hours	1	1.00**	91.3-94.4 million miles (147-152 million km)	—

* Venus rotates, or spins on its axis, once every 243 days. But its direction of rotation and the time it takes to orbit the Sun make a Venusian "day" – sunrise to sunrise – 117 Earth days long. ** Multiply your weight by this number to find out how much you would weigh on this planet.

Fact File: Uncovering the Shrouded Planet

Venus is the sixth largest known planet in our Solar System. The second closest planet to the Sun, Venus never travels very far away from the Sun. That is why it can only be seen just before the Sun rises or just after it sets. Venus is known as the Morning Star during its appearance before dawn, and the Evening Star during its appearance after dusk.

Venus is the brightest of all the planets and stars. Only the Sun and Earth's Moon are brighter. In fact, there have been reports of Venus's "shining" brightly enough on a moonless night to cast shadows on Earth!

More is known about Venus today than ever before. Beginning in the 1960s, probes have been studying the surface of Venus, its atmosphere, and its thick layer of clouds. It is this thick layer of clouds that obscures Venus's surface, gives the planet its bright appearance, and holds in the intense heat of the Sun. Due to probes, Venus is no longer thought of as Earth's mysterious "twin." Yet it remains one of the most beautiful and intriguing objects gracing the sky.

More Books about Venus

Journey to the Planets. Lauber (Crown)
Mars and the Inner Planets. Vogt (Franklin Watts)
On the Path of Venus: Discovering the Structure of Our Solar System. Motz (Pantheon)
Our Planetary System. Asimov (Gareth Stevens)
The Solar System. (National Geographic)
Venus, Near Neighbor of the Sun. Asimov (Lothrop, Lee & Shepard)

Videos

Our Solar System. (Gareth Stevens)
Venus: A Shrouded Mystery. (Gareth Stevens)

Places to Visit

You can explore Venus and other parts of the Universe without leaving Earth. Here are some museums and centers where you can find a variety of space exhibits.

Air and Space Museum
Smithsonian Institution
601 Independence Avenue SW
Washington, D.C. 20560

Henry Crown Science Center
Museum of Science and Industry
57th Street and Lake Shore Drive
Chicago, IL 60637

International Women's Air and Space Museum
One Chamber Plaza
Dayton, OH 45402

Edmonton Space and Science Centre
11211 - 142nd Street
Edmonton, Alberta K5M 4A1

Sydney Observatory
Observatory Hill
Sydney NSW 2000 Australia

Space and Rocket Center and Space Camp
One Tranquility Base
Huntsville, AL 35807

Places to Write

Here are some places you can write for more information about Venus. Be sure to state what kind of information you would like. Include your full name and address for a reply.

National Space Society
922 Pennsylvania Avenue SE
Washington, D.C. 20003

The Planetary Society
65 North Catalina
Pasadena, CA 91106

Canadian Space Agency
Communications Department
6767 Route de L'Aeroport
Saint Hubert, Quebec J3Y 8Y9

Anglo-Australian Observatory
P.O. Box 296
Epping, NSW 2121 Australia

Glossary

Aphrodite Terra: one of the two "continents" on Venus, named for Aphrodite, the ancient Greek goddess of love.

atmosphere: the layer of gases that surrounds a planet, star, or moon. The atmosphere of Venus is very dense, poisonous, and filled with lightning.

billion: the number represented by 1 followed by nine zeroes – 1,000,000,000. In some countries, this number is called "a thousand million." In these countries, one billion would then be represented by 1 followed by twelve zeroes – 1,000,000,000,000 – a million million.

carbon dioxide: a gas necessary for plant life. It is a colorless, heavy gas. Carbon dioxide is what gives soda its fizz. When humans and other animals breathe, they exhale carbon dioxide.

ellipse: an oval; the oval-shaped, or lopsided, orbit a planet makes around the Sun.

Evening Star: the name by which Venus has long been known when it appears in the evening sky.

greenhouse effect: the phenomenon whereby heat entering a planet's atmosphere becomes trapped and continues to build up until the surface temperature of the planet rises. It is thought to be responsible for Venus's being the hottest known body in the Solar System other than the Sun.

infrared radiation: "beneath the red" radiation. Infrared radiation is invisible to the naked eye, but it can be felt as heat.

Ishtar Terra: one of the two "continents" on Venus, named for the Babylonian goddess of love.

Lucifer: a Latin name meaning "bringer of light." It is applied to both Venus as the Morning Star (because it rises before the Sun) and to the devil (as the most glorious of angels before his fall).

Morning Star: the name by which Venus has long been known when it appears in the morning sky.

solar transit: the passing of a planet or other smaller celestial body across the disk, or face, of the Sun.

sulfuric acid: a corrosive liquid able to dissolve solid rock. It is found in Venus's atmosphere, making Venus one place where there is literally "acid rain."

Venus: the ancient Roman goddess of love. The planet Venus was named after her.

Index

Born in 1920, Isaac Asimov came to the United States as a young boy from his native Russia. As a young man, he was a student of biochemistry. In time, he became one of the most productive writers the world has ever known. His books cover a spectrum of topics, including science, history, language theory, fantasy, and science fiction. His brilliant imagination gained him the respect and admiration of adults and children alike. Sadly, Isaac Asimov died shortly after the publication of the first edition of *Isaac Asimov's Library of the Universe.*

The publishers wish to thank the following for permission to reproduce copyright material: front cover, © Sky and Space 1991; 4, © William P. Sterne, Jr.; 5, © Keith Ward 1990; 6-7 (lower), New Mexico State University Observatory; 8, 9 (inset), Yerkes Observatory; 9 (large), Courtesy of Crisp, Sinton, Ragent, Hodapp, 1989; 10, © MariLynn Flynn 1987; 10-11, © MariLynn Flynn 1990; 11 (both), NASA; 12, Naval Research Laboratory; 12-13, NASA; 13, © Paul Dimare 1990; 14, © David Hardy; 14-15 (upper), © MariLynn Flynn 1987; 14-15 (lower), © Sovfoto; 16, © Julian Baum 1990; 17 (large), © MariLynn Flynn 1987; 17 (inset), © Matthew Groshek 1980; 18 (upper), Yerkes Observatory; 18 (lower), Courtesy of Richard Baum; 18-19 (large), © Garret Moore 1990; 18-19 (inset), © Rick Karpinski/DeWalt and Associates; 20 (upper), © Sky and Space 1991; 20 (lower), NASA; 20-21, Jet Propulsion Laboratory; 21, NASA; ; 22-23 (upper), United States Geological Survey; 22-23 (lower), 24, Jet Propulsion Laboratory; 24-25, Greg Walz-Chojnacki; 25, 26, NASA; 26-27, Courtesy of Mitchell Park Conservatory; 27, © Garret Moore 1989; 28, © Thomas O. Miller/Studio "X"; 28-29, © Sally Bensusen.